From a heart of gratefulness, I thank you Lord for the grace bestowed upon me for this work of ministry to your daughters. A seed sown and cultivated over the past 20 years has inspired the content of this book. I pray that every young girl will see herself in any characters of the book and leave feeling strengthened and encouraged by these precious truths inspired by your word.

Your daughter, Tsia

This Book is Dedicated To:

_____

_____

_____

_____

_____

STRONG, BRAVE, GOD's GIRL

Written by: Tsia K. Jones

Faith on Display International
Alexandria, Virginia

Strong, Brave, God's Girl

Copyright © 2025 by Tsia K. Jones

To donate this book to encourage and inspire young girls around the world, visit www.equityfoundationinc.org

ISBN: 979-8-9930599-2-1
Library of Congress Control Number: 2025924971

Faith On Display International
5510 Cherokee Avenue Suite 300
Alexandria, VA 22312
www.faithondisplay.net

Dear Daughter, of the King,

Your Heavenly Father inspired this book and had you in mind. I want you to always know that Jesus loves and adores you!

The Lord teaches me in His Ways. I will meditate on His word in the day and night. I grow strong in God's word. Through the word I learn God's voice.

I flourish like a tree planted by a river of water. I am like a tree that has good fruit. I have the fruit of God's Spirit: Love, joy, peace, patience, kindness, goodness, faithfulness, gentleness and self-control.

The skies declare the work of God's hands. I am also the work of God's hands. God calls me His own. I can call on Him whenever I am in need. God will hear and answer me.

God is forever present and I can place my trust in Him. I declare, Jesus is my way, my truth, and my life. Jesus you are the only Way to the Father.

God will lead and guide me. He will lead me down the righteous path. It is God who establishes my steps. God's word is a lamp that lights my path.

I choose to follow Jesus for He is the Light of the world. His light in me shines and shall not be hidden. I am the light of the world. Darkness will not overcome Jesus' light in me.

I see the work of God's fingers in the stars. He has created the stars and calls each one by name. God also calls me by name. When I hear God call my name, I will answer Him. I will say, "Here I am. Speak Lord your servant is listening."

I am His sheep and I know His voice. I will obey His voice and follow His commandments. The Lord gives me commands and laws to keep me safe.

God has made me wonderfully and with great honor. His thoughts of me are as much as the sand by the seashore. I am the apple of His eye. God's eyes and heart are always with me. His Holy Spirit lives within me.

God loves me deeply and beyond measure. I choose to love Him more than anything in this world. God has called me out of the world. I am set apart for His purpose and plans. I will always honor and respect God's presence in my life.

I put on the whole armor of God so that I may stand strong. God will teach me how to fight His way. The word of God is my sword. I fight from a position of victory. It is Jesus who gives me the victory. He will make even my enemies to be at peace with me.

He is strong when I am weak. God will not put more on me than I can endure. He is present whenever I need help.

When I ask, what is wrong with me? God instead You see all that is right with me. I can call out to God when I am afraid. God will protect and keep me from harm. God has not given me the spirit of fear but power, love, and a clear mind.

I trust God will work everything together for my good because I love Him. God has called me to fulfill His purpose in the earth. When I ask, God will reveal my purpose to me.

The beautiful lilies and the birds above remind me of God's care and love for His creation. He clothes the lilies in the field and feeds the birds of the air. So, I do not have to worry about my life.

God provides everything that I need. He is a good father who gives me good gifts. I will believe God's promises and trust Him to perform them. I can trust God will do what He said.

I will not forget all the good things that God does for me. I will think about things that are true, right, pure, and lovely. I will keep my mind on these things. God can do exceedingly and abundantly above all I can ask, think or imagine.

I will express my gratitude by thanking God every day for all the good things in my life. It is the Lord who makes me glad. I will rejoice in the Lord always!

I will serve God with all of my heart. God blesses me with gifts, I am to use to serve others. I am also a precious gift that is sacred and protected. As rubies or diamonds are cherished, I will protect what is pure and precious about me.

I will remain encouraged in doing good and never give up. I am the hands and feet of Jesus in the world. The Lord can depend on me to carry out His plans in the earth.

I am not alone in this journey. God is for me and has plans to do good things for me. He dearly loves me and adores me. God has chosen me and made me His holy offspring.

He goes before me and will never leave me or throw me away. God will be with me wherever I go. I will always remind myself that, God's got me!

I am Strong.
I am Brave.
I am God's Girl.

Jesus is the Lion of Judah who fights for me. I will call on Jesus when I am in trouble. He will rescue me from all my troubles. Jesus is a good shepherd who protects His sheep. I am Jesus' sheep and He will never lose me.

I will not fear because He makes me strong and brave. I will say to myself every day Strong Girl, Brave Girl, God's Girl.

Prayer of Salvation

Heavenly Father, I believe Jesus Christ is the Son of God who died for my sins. I confess my sins and ask for forgiveness. I receive Jesus today as my Lord and Savior. Lord Jesus, I ask that you come into my heart and fill me with your precious Holy Spirit.

By the confession of my mouth, I believe I am saved. Lord Jesus, thank you for the gift of salvation.

www.ingramcontent.com/pod-product-compliance
Lightning Source LLC
Chambersburg PA
CBHW041605120626
46551CB00002B/322